Into The Light
MINISTRIES

intothelightministries.ca

Copyright ©2025 by Into The Light Ministries

All rights reserved.

No part of this publication may be reproduced, distributed, or transmitted in any form or by any means, including photocopying, recording, or other electronic or mechanical methods, without the prior written permission of the publisher, except as permitted by U.S. copyright law. For permission requests, contact Into The Light Ministries at intothelightministries.ca

Unless otherwise indicated, Scripture quotations are from the *ESV® Bible (The Holy Bible, English Standard Version®)*, copyright © 2001 by Crossway, a publishing ministry of Good News Publishers. All rights reserved.

ISBN: 9798315996095

Into The Light Documentary

From Bondage in Sin to Freedom in Christ

A Seven Chapter Group Study
On Freedom From Pornography

Into The Light Ministries

Table of Contents

Introduction for Leading Groups to Freedom   **5**

CHAPTER 1	Jeremy Pierre on Sexual Sin And Its Consequences	**12**
CHAPTER 2	Jenny Solomon on God's Design For Sexuality	**26**
CHAPTER 3	Heath Lambert on Understanding The Heart	**40**
CHAPTER 4	Deepak Reju on The Practical Radical Measures	**52**
CHAPTER 5	Ellen Dykas on Running With Endurance	**64**
CHAPTER 6	Garrett Kell on True Freedom In The Church	**76**
CHAPTER 7	David Platt on Pornography And Missions	**88**

Next Steps   **100**

Introduction for Leading Groups to Freedom

Thank you for using this workbook to dive deeper into the *Into The Light* documentary and video series. Whether you are using this resource in a Bible study, small group, discipleship relationship, counseling room, or accountability context, we are grateful for your kingdom work.

If you are here because of your own struggle with pornography, know that you are not beyond hope. Sexual sin thrives in the dark, but change begins when you step into the light. We would encourage you to ask a friend, parent, or pastor to work through the study with you. No matter how long you've struggled, God's grace is greater still. Jesus came for sinners (Luke 5:32), and if you are in Christ, you are a new creation (2 Corinthians 5:17). You have a good Father who cares for his children (Psalm 103:13). He does not break a bruised reed (Isaiah 42:3). He knows your past and present sins, yet he moves towards you in Christ (Romans 5:8). You are not alone in this fight. Freedom is possible.

If you are here to help others, praise God! You have a critical role to play. Sexual sin is often shameful, heavy, and complex, and those who are struggling with sin need someone to offer grace, accountability, and truth. Thank you for taking on this role.

For each episode of the film, we have two sets of questions. The first set is intended to facilitate group discussion and enable you to dig deeper into the series. We hope that all group members are open and vulnerable. The second set of questions is intended to be taken home and used for personal reflection. If you are using this series in a counseling relationship, consider using these reflection questions as a tool for counseling homework. Before diving in, we want to offer some recommendations on how to lead a group discussion.

First, prepare beforehand to guide the conversation. You cannot change the hearts of those in your group, but your preparation can make a huge difference in helping the material impact each individual.

1. Prepare in Advance: Review each session's discussion questions ahead of time. Pray over the material and consider how it applies to your own life. Consider highlighting particular questions you want to spend the majority of your time on. Don't feel obligated to use every question.
2. Ask Open-Ended Questions: Encourage deeper thinking by asking questions that invite reflection, not just yes/no answers.
3. Be Prepared for Silence: Some questions will be met with hesitation or silence. That's okay. Give space for people to process and think of an answer. Don't rush to fill the silence.
4. Manage Time Wisely: Be mindful of the clock, ensuring there is time for both teaching and discussion. There will be times when you need to gently steer the conversation back to the main topic.
5. Keep Each Other Accountable: Consider incorporating an accountability portion into your meetings that could live on beyond the seven weeks of the video series. This provides a time for confession, repentance, and encouragement as participants grow and kill sin.
6. Pray Diligently: Pray for wisdom as you lead, for soft hearts in the group, for the Spirit to work powerfully, and for long-term freedom from pornography.

Second, set the tone of the discussion. The atmosphere you cultivate will significantly influence the depth and vulnerability of the discussions. Aim to create a space marked by grace, truth, and genuine care. Here are principles to keep in mind:

1. Lead with Vulnerability: Model openness by sharing your own story and questions. When leaders are authentic, they help others be honest as well. We would encourage you to begin week one with a time of confession where everyone shares their story and/or reasons for coming to the group.
2. Keep the Gospel Central: Every meeting should be characterized by the hope of the gospel, not fear, shame, or dismissiveness. Take time each week to remember Christ's heart for sinners and the great hope we have in him.
3. Encourage Personal Reflection: Remind participants to engage with the take-home questions and spend time in prayer and Scripture reading between sessions.
4. Avoid Cultural Commentary: Encourage your group to speak with the language of "I" and "me," *not* "we" and "they." The primary focus of this study is to fight sexual sin in our *own* lives, not to offer an analysis on "we as Christians" or the "dangers of pornography".
5. Recognize the Gravity: Remind participants that sexual sin is not trivial (Proverbs 6:27). We need to take our sin seriously and fight like our lives depend on it (Matthew 18:9).

Third, navigate pornography-specific challenges. Caring for those in your group who are addicted to pornography can be challenging and complex. Here are some key principles to keep in mind:

1. Cut Off Access ASAP: An effective way to extinguish a fire is removing its source of fuel, and the same is true with pornography. It is vital to quickly set up restrictions and safeguards to cut off access to explicit content. Chapter four of the documentary explains *why* cutting off access is needed, and our *TechSafe* series explains *how* to cut off access to pornography on every device you may own. The *TechSafe* series is available on our website.
2. Be Careful With Specifics: Encourage participants to speak in general terms of ways they are tempted to sin but to avoid sharing the specific name of any websites, apps, shows, or books. These details may end up tempting others in the group. Be ready to jump in if something inappropriate is being shared.
3. Follow-up: It can be easy to make commitments to cut off access and fight sin in a group, but hard to truly live it out when alone. Love your brother or sister by following up with them throughout the week to encourage and hold them accountable.
4. Get to the Heart: Cutting off access to pornography is a necessary first step to change, but it is ultimately useless if there is not also heart change. Help participants understand what may be underneath their struggle with pornography and how God's word addresses those desires, fears, and needs.
5. Handle Disclosures with Care: Pornography addictions are often wrapped up in other broken situations. If someone shares a particularly painful experience like abuse or temptation to suicide, respond with compassion. Thank members of your group for sharing and follow up privately to offer additional support and resources. It may be prudent to quickly connect them to a biblical counselor.

6. Be Patient: Sometimes, God works change very quickly. However, more often, the process of breaking free from pornography takes time. Remember that they are seeking to reorient their hearts and retrain their bodies to obedience. It takes time for both the heart and the brain to create new pathways of righteousness.
7. Beware of Excuses: It can be challenging to discern real repentance from faulty repentance. One key distinguisher is whether the individual makes excuses for their sin or takes responsibility for it. It is easier to blame shift than to face personal sin. Patterns of excuses and an unwillingness to accept the consequences should raise significant alarm bells. In some cases, this may even reveal that the man or woman is not truly saved.
8. Remember that Sex is a Good Gift: It can be easy in a discussion about pornography to foster a negative view of sexuality. It is vital to know that sex is not bad; sex outside God's design is. Within God's boundaries, our sexuality is a good gift to be celebrated and embraced. If you want to dig deeper into this topic as a group, you can watch Andrew Walker's two episodes in the *Parenting & Pornography* video series on our website.
9. Involve Your Church: The Christian life is not meant to be lived alone. As you begin this study, let your pastor know you are starting this group. Consider inviting other church members to do it with you. If anyone in the group is not involved in a gospel-preaching church, encourage them to find one.
10. Remember the Basics: It can be tempting to feel like we need to move past the basics of the Christian life to make progress in fighting pornography. In reality, it is in daily choices of faith and repentance that true change happens (Ecclesiastes 12:13). Help participants remember the basics.

Leading this group may feel overwhelming. Remember that it is God who changes hearts, not us. Leading the group is not about perfection; it's about seeking to be faithful (1 Corinthians 4:2). Trust that God will use your efforts to impact hearts and lives for his glory. You are part of a larger story where God is restoring marriages, building his church, setting sinners free from bondage (Colossians 1:13-14), and reuniting humanity to himself in Christ (Colossians 1:20).

Thank you for your leadership, faithfulness, and heart to serve. May God bless you as you help others through sexual sin towards change and God's glory.

In Christ,
John-Michael Bout and Jacob Valk
Executive Directors of Into The Light Ministries
@aboutjem @itsthevalk @intothelight_ministries

Sexual Sin And Its Consequences

Chapter One – Jeremy Pierre

Group Study: Week 1

START HERE

In chapter one, Jeremy addresses the consequences of pornography in daily life and its destructive effects on the heart. He illustrates the deep destruction of pornography and offers Gospel grace for struggling sinners. He shows how behind every temptation is the promise of something good and how it is helpful to look at what 'goods' are most tempting for us to pursue apart from God's design.

Before watching the episode, **take time to open in prayer and read the following passages**:

> 1 John 2:15–17
> "Do not love the world or the things in the world. If anyone loves the world, the love of the Father is not in him. For all that is in the world—the desires of the flesh and the desires of the eyes and pride of life—is not from the Father but is from the world. And the world is passing away along with its desires, but whoever does the will of God abides forever."

> Psalm 32:5
> "I acknowledged my sin to you, and I did not cover my iniquity; I said, "I will confess my transgressions to the LORD," and you forgave the iniquity of my sin."

SCAN TO WATCH

intothelightministries.ca

KEY IDEAS

1. Sin seeks good apart from God's design.

2. Porn is never victimless or harmless.

3. The sin of pornography distorts the way we see and act in the world.

4. Guilt is a gift from God when it is calibrated rightly.

NOTES

GROUP STUDY QUESTIONS

1. What is one thing that encouraged or challenged you from Jeremy's talk?

2. What good things does porn pretend to be? Or put another way, if porn could speak, what would be the good news promise it would make to you?

3. Jeremy describes porn as "trickery... an imaginary world of false goods that cuts you off from the genuine world of real goods." What do you think he means? What real goods does porn's false goods keep you from?

4. We can be tempted to believe that pornography is a harmless and private sin. Who and how are other people affected when you watch pornography?

> Your family
> Your spouse
> Your church
> Your friends
> Your witness to unbelievers
> Your relationship with self
> Your relationship with God
> Your brain
> Your desire for God's word
> Your desire to pray

5. Jeremy talked about "the desires of the flesh and the desires of the eyes and the pride of life." In light of this text from 1 John, what does it mean that porn has a way of conditioning and training you? How does this affect the way you act?

> **1 John 2:15–17**
> "Do not love the world or the things in the world. If anyone loves the world, the love of the Father is not in him. For all that is in the world—the desires of the flesh and the desires of the eyes and pride of life—is not from the Father but is from the world. And the world is passing away along with its desires, but whoever does the will of God abides forever."

6. What other things can be lusted after like porn, but might not be considered pornography in a technical sense? How might Instagram, movies, novels, VR, video games, and other forms of media be unhelpful?

7. How can you handle guilt from sin rightly? How can you handle guilt from sin wrongly? Consider confessing sin together in prayer through Psalm 32.

> **Psalm 32:5**
> "I acknowledged my sin to you, and I did not cover my iniquity; I said, "I will confess my transgressions to the LORD," and you forgave the iniquity of my sin."

8. Pornography is incredibly addictive. How should we think about sin as addiction while recognizing that we are still responsible for our sinful actions and desires? How do these addictions use and twist God's good design for sexuality?

TAKE HOME QUESTIONS FOR FURTHER REFLECTION

1. Have you ever genuinely asked God to give you eyes to see the evil of pornography?

2. Do you believe, deep down, that God is denying you something good by forbidding pornography? How do God's commands align with his designs? How does God's good character assure that his commands are always best?

3. What are some of the contributing factors that have led to your seeking out sexual sin? Are there issues in your past? Consider these questions to help think through your past and be specific in answering them:

   - How are you reacting wrongly to your past circumstances?
   - Do you blame your past for your present sin?
   - How are you reacting rightly to your past circumstances?
   - What are you currently desiring most?

4. Do you try to find security, affirmation, freedom, love, or escape in porn? What desires lie underneath your pursuit of porn? How does porn fail to provide those things? How does Jesus offer you all of these in the gospel?

5. Do you have an appropriate level of guilt? How can you direct your guilt to bring you to Christ rather than to despair? Make a list of how you can handle guilt from sin rightly and another list of how you can handle guilt from sin wrongly. Take time to ask the Lord to help you in this area.

KEY SCRIPTURES

- 1 John 2:15–17

- Psalm 32:5

RECOMMENDED RESOURCES

- *The Dynamic Heart in Daily Life* by Jeremy Pierre

- *The Mortification of Sin* by John Owen

- *Addictions: A Banquet in the Grave* by Ed Welch

- Get a discount on Accountable2You using the link: a2u.app/IntoTheLight

- Get a discount on Covenant Eyes using the code: INTOTHELIGHT

- Other Into The Light Resources: intothelightministries.ca

God's Design For Sexuality

Chapter Two – Jenny Solomon

Group Study: Week 2

START HERE

In chapter two, Jenny addresses God's good design for our sexuality and the importance of having a positive view of sex. She also offers the grace of Jesus Christ to sinners who have broken God's good design and struggle to find hope.

Before watching the episode, **take time to open in prayer and read the following passages**:

> ### Hebrews 4:14-16
> "Since then we have a great high priest who has passed through the heavens, Jesus, the Son of God, let us hold fast our confession. For we do not have a high priest who is unable to sympathize with our weaknesses, but one who in every respect has been tempted as we are, yet without sin. Let us then with confidence draw near to the throne of grace, that we may receive mercy and find grace to help in time of need."

> ### Romans 5:1-6
> "Therefore, since we have been justified by faith, we have peace with God through our Lord Jesus Christ. Through him we have also obtained access by faith into this grace in which we stand, and we rejoice in hope of the glory of God. Not only that, but we rejoice in our sufferings, knowing that suffering produces endurance, and endurance produces character, and character produces hope, and hope does not put us to shame, because God's love has been poured into our hearts through the Holy Spirit who has been given to us. For while we were still weak, at the right time Christ died for the ungodly."

SCAN TO WATCH

intothelightministries.ca

KEY IDEAS

1. God designed all sexual activity to be enjoyed in the context of marriage.

2. There is sexual brokenness in this world and in me.

3. God has designed boundaries within which your sexuality can flourish and outside of which you will wither.

4. Masturbation does not fit God's design for sexuality.

5. Jesus moves towards sinners in their brokenness.

NOTES

GROUP STUDY QUESTIONS

1. What is one thing that encouraged or challenged you from Jenny's talk?

2. How were you first taught about sex and marriage? (Was it through the church, school, family, porn, media, etc.?) Was this consistent or inconsistent with a biblical understanding of sex?

3. Consider these five main boundaries of God's design for sex. How does masturbation fall outside this good design? How does God's good design for sex within covenant marriage promise something *better* than masturbation?

- Sex is to be enjoyed within the covenantal boundaries of marriage.
- Sex is for cultivating emotional, physical, and spiritual intimacy between spouses.
- Sex is for the selfless giving and receiving of pleasure.
- Sex is for bringing new life into the world.
- Sex is intended to offer insight into Christ's relationship with the church.

- Masturbation does not happen within the context of marriage.
- Masturbation does not cultivate intimacy between spouses.
- Masturbation selfishly takes, focuses on the individual's needs, and fosters lust.
- Masturbation cannot bring children into the world.
- Masturbation is a significant distortion of the Christ-church relationship.

4. According to Hebrews 4:14-16, how is Jesus ministering to his people right now in heaven? How does this encourage you in fighting sin in general and pornography specifically?

> "Since then we have a great high priest who has passed through the heavens, Jesus, the Son of God, let us hold fast our confession. For we do not have a high priest who is unable to sympathize with our weaknesses, but one who in every respect has been tempted as we are, yet without sin. Let us then with confidence draw near to the throne of grace, that we may receive mercy and find grace to help in time of need."

5. "Sex is good!" What thoughts come to mind when you read that statement? When the culture says, "sex is good," how does this differ from what Jenny means?

6. Jenny said, "we can both hold onto our standards for God's good design and have compassion for those who have broken it." Have you felt this tension anywhere in your life?

7. How do you respond after you sin ? What do these reactions reveal about your perspective of God and yourself?

- Self-righteousness
- Excuses
- Pride,
- Shame
- Hopelessness
- Trust
- Repentance
- Confession
- Sorrow
- Worship

TAKE HOME QUESTIONS FOR FURTHER REFLECTION

1. Were your parents married? What example did they set for you? How has this shaped your perspective of marriage?

2. Have you struggled with masturbation? How did you first discover it? Is masturbation a coping mechanism for anything?

3. Are you tempted to believe you have to clean yourself up before approaching the Lord? How does Romans 5:6 address this?

> "Christ showed his love for us, in that while we were still sinners, Christ died for us."

4. Jenny ends with a challenging question: "Do you really believe God has the power to save you?" Evaluate your own heart. Do you believe this? What makes you have doubts?

5. "Desperation can lead to hopelessness or it can cause us to repent." How are you practically going to take steps this week to move from hopelessness to repentance?

KEY SCRIPTURES

- Hebrews 4:12-5:2

- Romans 5:1-9

- Luke 7:36-50

RECOMMENDED RESOURCES

- *Redeem Your Marriage* by Jenny Solomon

- *Gentle and Lowly* by Dane Ortlund

- *Marriage and The Family: Biblical Essentials* by Andreas Köstenberger with David W. Jones

- Get a discount on Accountable2You using the link: a2u.app/IntoTheLight

- Get a discount on Covenant Eyes using the code: INTOTHELIGHT

- Other Into The Light Resources: intothelightministries.ca

Into The Light
MINISTRIES

Understanding The Heart

Chapter Three – Heath Lambert

Group Study: Week 3

START HERE

In chapter three, Heath Lambert addresses the complexities of the heart and offers key tools to identify the sinful desires beneath pornography. He discusses confession, sorrow, accountability, triggers, and the root of sin. Heart work takes time and careful attention.

Before watching the episode, **take time to open in prayer and read the following passages**:

> James 1:13–15
> "Let no one say when he is tempted, "I am being tempted by God," for God cannot be tempted with evil, and he himself tempts no one. But each person is tempted when he is lured and enticed by his own desire. Then desire when it has conceived gives birth to sin, and sin when it is fully grown brings forth death."

> 2 Corinthians 7:9–11
> "As it is, I rejoice, not because you were grieved, but because you were grieved into repenting. For you felt a godly grief, so that you suffered no loss through us. For godly grief produces a repentance that leads to salvation without regret, whereas worldly grief produces death. For see what earnestness this godly grief has produced in you, but also what eagerness to clear yourselves, what indignation, what fear, what longing, what zeal, what punishment! At every point you have proved yourselves innocent in the matter."

SCAN TO WATCH

intothelightministries.ca

KEY IDEAS

1. Your main problem with pornography is not that it exists in your life but that your heart desires it.

2. The root, shoot, and fruit metaphor will help you understand your heart.

3. In order to overcome the sin of pornography, you must address the root (desires) of the sin.

4. Knowing what triggers you can help you better understand your heart.

5. True repentance confesses sin to both God and others, and is willing to accept the consequences.

NOTES

GROUP STUDY QUESTIONS

1. What is one thing that encouraged or challenged you from Heath's talk?

2. Heath used the dandelion metaphor to explain James 1:13-15. What does this passage teach us about temptation, desire, and sin?

James 1:13–15

"Let no one say when he is tempted, 'I am being tempted by God,' for God cannot be tempted with evil, and he himself tempts no one. But each person is tempted when he is lured and enticed by his own desire. Then desire when it has conceived gives birth to sin, and sin when it is fully grown brings forth death."

Fruit — The Results of Sin

Shoot — The Sinful Action

Root — Heart Desires

3. Heath shared a practical question to get to the center of our hearts: "What are you wanting so badly you will sin to get it and sin if you don't get it?" Do you find this question helpful? Why or why not?

4. How do our triggers to sin reveal what we want? What are some things that might trigger someone to think lustfully or watch porn?

5. How do past influences shape your present struggle with pornography? Where did your sin and personal responsibility begin in your story? What parts of your story were you not able to control that should be lamented?

Sinful Heart Response	External Circumstances
What I Could Control	*What I Couldn't Control*
• Pride	• Events
• Sexual sin	• Persons
• Lust	• Lack of knowledge
• Escapism	• Accidental Exposure
• Idolatry	• False Teaching
• Lying	• Unmet Needs
• Fearing man	• External Pressure

6. Read 2 Corinthians 7:10-11. What is worldly sorrow versus godly sorrow? What is grief meant to lead to?

> 2 Corinthians 7:9–11
> "As it is, I rejoice, not because you were grieved, but because you were grieved into repenting. For you felt a godly grief, so that you suffered no loss through us. For godly grief produces a repentance that leads to salvation without regret, whereas worldly grief produces death. For see what earnestness this godly grief has produced in you, but also what eagerness to clear yourselves, what indignation, what fear, what longing, what zeal, what punishment! At every point you have proved yourselves innocent in the matter."

7. What motivates you towards repentance? Are your desires to change your actions (shoot) more motivated by not liking the outcomes of sin (fruit) rather than loving, obeying, honoring, and enjoying God (root)?

8. What is one step you can take this week to better understand your heart?

TAKE HOME QUESTIONS FOR FURTHER REFLECTION

1. Have you tried to address the shoot (action) of sexual sin without addressing the root (heart desires)? How might you now address the root?

2. Are your actions the fruit of godly repentance or merely a desire to avoid consequences and shame?

3. Identify 3-5 triggers in your life. What do they reveal about your underlying desires? Do you see any patterns in your heart desires?

4. Heath says one of the first steps of godly grief is to reach out for help. Are you willing to be completely honest with a fellow believer about your sin? Can you identify one person you will call today?

KEY SCRIPTURES

- James 1:13

- 2 Corinthians 7:9-11

- Ephesians 5:13-14

RECOMMENDED RESOURCES

- *Finally Free* by Heath Lambert

- *How People Change* by Timothy Lane and Paul David Tripp

- *The Doctrine of Repentance* by Thomas Watson

- Get a discount on Accountable2You using the link: a2u.app/IntoTheLight

- Get a discount on Covenant Eyes using the code: INTOTHELIGHT

- Other Into The Light Resources: intothelightministries.ca

Into The Light
MINISTRIES

The Practical Radical Measures

Chapter Four – Deepak Reju

Group Study: Week 4

START HERE

In chapter four, Deepak addresses the need to radically cut off access to pornography. If you have not already cut off access to explicit material, head over to our *TechSafe* series, where we walk through this process in detail. Deepak also speaks on why prayer, Scripture reading, and memorization are vital tools to fight pornography.

Before watching the episode, **take time to open in prayer and read the following passages**:

Matthew 5:27-30

"You have heard that it was said, 'You shall not commit adultery.' But I say to you that everyone who looks at a woman with lustful intent has already committed adultery with her in his heart. If your right eye causes you to sin, tear it out and throw it away. For it is better that you lose one of your members than that your whole body be thrown into hell. And if your right hand causes you to sin, cut it off and throw it away. For it is better that you lose one of your members than that your whole body go into hell."

Psalm 1:1-3

"Blessed is the man who walks not in the counsel of the wicked, nor stands in the way of sinners, nor sits in the seat of scoffers; but his delight is in the law of the LORD, and on his law he meditates day and night. He is like a tree planted by streams of water that yields its fruit in its season, and its leaf does not wither. In all that he does, he prospers."

SCAN TO WATCH

intothelightministries.ca

KEY IDEAS

1. Jesus is radical in his approach toward sin.

2. You have to protect yourself from yourself.

3. Behind sin lies a false theology of God.

4. God's word is fundamental to fighting pornography.

5. Even though sexual sin is ultimately a heart issue, we do not abandon practical measures.

6. Find an accessible person other than yourself to be the administrator for your devices.

NOTES

GROUP STUDY QUESTIONS

1. What is one thing that encouraged or challenged you from Deepak's talk?

2. Are there any devices in this room right now that you could find pornography on? How can those devices be locked down to prevent access? Consider using our TechSafe series to learn how to shut down your device ASAP.

3. "You have to protect yourself from yourself." Do you agree with this statement? Why or why not?

4. Do you typically approach the battle through introspection (examining your heart) or by trying to cut off access more? Which of these has been most helpful to you?

5. Read Psalm 119:9 and discuss Don Whitney's tea bag analogy about Scripture meditation. What is the difference between Scripture meditation and simply reading? How can you personally utilize God's Word in your active fight against sin?

> "How can a young man keep his way pure? By guarding it according to your word."

6. Has praying with others been a regular part of your Christian walk and fight against sin? Consider breaking off into groups of two or three right now and praying for each other for a few minutes. Beginning the rhythm of praying with and for one another can be transformative in the battle against porn.

7. Read Psalm 1. What does it look like to become a Psalm 1 man or woman?

> "Blessed is the man who walks not in the counsel of the wicked, nor stands in the way of sinners, nor sits in the seat of scoffers; but his delight is in the law of the LORD, and on his law he meditates day and night. He is like a tree planted by streams of water that yields its fruit in its season, and its leaf does not wither. In all that he does, he prospers. The wicked are not so, but are like chaff that the wind drives away. Therefore the wicked will not stand in the judgment, nor sinners in the congregation of the righteous; for the LORD knows the way of the righteous, but the way of the wicked will perish."

8. Good accountability is regular, accessible, honest about sin, severe on sin, has a mature presence, and has the goal of total freedom from sexual sin. Why do we find it so hard to practice this accountability?

9. What is one change you need to make this week?

TAKE HOME QUESTIONS FOR FURTHER REFLECTION

1. What radical measures are you going to take to cut off access to pornography? Are those radical enough?

2. When are you going to implement these radical measures? Is that soon enough?

3. Who are you going to ask to help you with this? Are they available and qualified?

4. Do you have a workaround on your phone? Who knows about it? Who will you tell?

5. Reflect on the last time you gave into sexual sin. Try to remember what you were thinking. Did you have a boundary in place to block that temptation? What did you believe about God? What desire were you seeking to fulfill?

6. Are there patterns to where and when you are sinfully acting out? Consider keeping a temptation journal for a week to help you track commonalities. Include the time, location, length, result, and heart desires you felt.

KEY SCRIPTURES

- Psalm 1

- Psalm 119:9-11

- Matthew 5:27-30

RECOMMENDED RESOURCES

- *Rescue Plan and Rescue Skills*
  by Deepak Reju and Jonathan Holmes

- *Pornography: Fighting for Purity (31-Day Devotional)*
  by Deepak Reju

- *Spiritual Disciplines for the Christian Life* by Donald Whitney

- Get a discount on Accountable2You using the link: a2u.app/IntoTheLight

- Get a discount on Covenant Eyes using the code: INTOTHELIGHT

- Other Into The Light Resources: intothelightministries.ca

Running With Endurance

Chapter Five – Ellen Dykas

Group Study: Week 5

START HERE

In chapter five, Ellen addresses those who may feel jaded in the battle against pornography and offers hope to those who fail. She also dissects some of the common temptations faced in fighting sin for the long haul. After years of pursuing holiness, falling, getting back up, and doing it all over again, it can be very easy to feel weary. This life is a marathon, and to run it well, we need God-dependent endurance.

Before watching the episode, **take time to open in prayer and read the following passages**:

Hebrews 12:1-2

"Therefore, since we are surrounded by so great a cloud of witnesses, let us also lay aside every weight, and sin which clings so closely, and let us run with endurance the race that is set before us, looking to Jesus, the founder and perfecter of our faith, who for the joy that was set before him endured the cross, despising the shame, and is seated at the right hand of the throne of God."

Romans 2:4

"Or do you presume on the riches of his kindness and forbearance and patience, not knowing that God's kindness is meant to lead you to repentance?"

SCAN TO WATCH

intothelightministries.ca

KEY IDEAS

1. Your fight against pornography is a marathon.

2. You do not belong to yourself; you belong to Jesus.

3. Resist the urge to let your track record become bigger in your heart than Jesus.

4. We have a merciful Savior who knows that sin will remain while we are in this world.

5. Resist the devil, and he will flee from you.

NOTES

GROUP STUDY QUESTIONS

1. What is one thing that encouraged or challenged you from Ellen's talk?

2. Setbacks in the fight for sexual integrity can lead to feeling jaded and apathetic. Are you tempted to believe any of these lies below? What new lies might you believe if you fall back into pornography?

   - That God does not exist.
   - That his design for sexuality includes porn.
   - That you are not a Christian.
   - That you will never get free.
   - That you can compartmentalize that part of life.
   - That taking your own life would be easier.
   - That porn is the only issue they have.
   - That you are too far gone.
   - That sinning only occasionally is okay.

3. Read Hebrews 12:1-2. Have you grown tired of resisting temptation and felt like giving up? What hope does this passage offer you? How does the gospel fuel your endurance?

> "Therefore, since we are surrounded by so great a cloud of witnesses, let us also lay aside every weight, and sin which clings so closely, and let us run with endurance the race that is set before us, looking to Jesus, the founder and perfecter of our faith, who for the joy that was set before him endured the cross, despising the shame, and is seated at the right hand of the throne of God."

4. Have you considered how addictive pornography is? If so, how can this impact your approach to fighting it?

5. Ellen says, "Resist the urge to let your track record become bigger in your heart than Jesus." Do you think this encourages a low view of sin? What is helpful about the statement?

6. Do you tend to use passive language when talking about watching porn? What does this reveal about your perspective of sin?

> "The language we use about our sin often reveals a passive mindset. Phrases like "I fell," "I slipped up," and "that sucked," can reveal that we are distancing ourselves from personal responsibility. Another way we do this is by using stories to mask or build sympathy for our sinful actions. God's word invites us to put to death passivity and excuse-making (Romans 8:13, Matthew 5:29-30)."

7. What are some Bible verses that you can take hold of when you are feeling broken by sin? Take time to brainstorm passages as a group.

8. Ellen invites us to recommit to the fundamentals of change discussed in the previous chapters. How would you sum up where we have been so far?

TAKE HOME QUESTIONS FOR FURTHER REFLECTION

1. The fight against sexual sin comes one day at a time. How can you pursue faithfulness *today*?

2. Can you think of ways you have sugar-coated or been less than honest in telling your accountability partner about your sin in the past? Do you need to apologize to them because of this?

3. Ellen gives a list of Scriptural truths that she calls "gentle reminders." Based on this list:

   - Do you believe there is no longer condemnation for you who are in Christ?
   - Do you believe that God is generous to extend forgiveness no matter how many times you fall?
   - Do you believe God shows mercy to those broken by sin?
   - Do you believe he is kind?
   - Is one of these promises from Scripture particularly hard for you to believe or remember?

Take time to thank the Lord for all the promises we have in Christ.

4. How can you grow in your understanding of God's kindness, forbearance, and patience? How can you grow to see your ability to repent as a loving gift from God and not a condemning burden? Take time to pray for the Lord's help in this area.

5. Are there steps from chapters 1-4 that you would like to recommit yourself to? Think through ways that you can move towards doing them.

KEY SCRIPTURES

- Hebrews 12:1-2
- Romans 2:4
- Psalm 51
- James 4:7
- 1 Peter 1
- Revelation 21:45

RECOMMENDED RESOURCES

- *Sexual Sanity For Women* by Ellen Dykas
- *Purity is Possible* by Helen Thorne
- *Shame: Being Known and Loved (31-Day Devotional)* by Esther Liu
- Get a discount on Accountable2You using the link: a2u.app/IntoTheLight
- Get a discount on Covenant Eyes using the code: INTOTHELIGHT
- Other Into The Light Resources: intothelightministries.ca

Into The Light
MINISTRIES

True Freedom In The Church

Chapter Six — Garrett Kell

Group Study: Week 6

START HERE

In chapter six, Garrett Kell addresses what true, joyful freedom looks like in the context of community. He paints a picture of our final hope and the glory of Christ's return as we press on in the daily battle. Encourage the group to apply the teaching to their local church context. Consider closing your time by praying for opportunities to share your freedom and victories with others.

Before watching the episode, **take time to open in prayer and read the following passages**:

> Matthew 5:8
> "Blessed are the pure in heart, for they shall see God."

> 1 Corinthians 6:9–11
> "Or do you not know that the unrighteous will not inherit the kingdom of God? Do not be deceived: neither the sexually immoral, nor idolaters, nor adulterers, nor men who practice homosexuality, nor thieves, nor the greedy, nor drunkards, nor revilers, nor swindlers will inherit the kingdom of God. And such were some of you. But you were washed, you were sanctified, you were justified in the name of the Lord Jesus Christ and by the Spirit of our God."

SCAN TO WATCH

intothelightministries.ca

KEY IDEAS

1. Sin promises pleasure but always hides the price tag.

2. You will never regret resisting sin but will always regret giving in.

3. The Christian life is more about direction than perfection.

4. The pure in heart will see God.

5. No one can take your joy from you when it is in Christ.

6. True freedom is eternal freedom.

NOTES

GROUP STUDY QUESTIONS

1. What is one thing that encouraged or challenged you from Garret's talk?

2. Garrett said, "You will never regret resisting sin. But you will always regret giving in." Can you give a personal example of this?

3. What is the promise of Mathew 5:8 for those who resist sin by grace and continue in purity? How might focusing on this outcome motivate you more than focusing on the consequences of the sin?

> "Blessed are the pure in heart, for they shall see God."

4. What practical steps did Garrett take when he was scrolling social media and came across a tempting image? What steps had Garrett clearly taken *before* that moment of temptation that allowed him to make the choice he did?

5. The church is not only a strategy for fighting sin, it is *essential* to the Christian life. Are God's people a key part of your Christian walk? How does committing to a local church help you in your fight against pornography?

6. How can dwelling on the future return of Christ help you see as well as fight against sin right now?

7. What is something you are grateful to God for this week as you fight this sin?

TAKE HOME QUESTIONS FOR FURTHER REFLECTION

1. Do you believe freedom from pornography is possible for you? What does your answer reveal about your perspective of God's grace in your life?

2. If, over the last few weeks (or months), you have had victory over porn, have you replaced it with any other sin? How can you apply the biblical principles you learned from the documentary to help you kill that sin?

3. If you are experiencing freedom, what are you going to do with it? How can you use your victories (even small ones) to motivate, disciple, and encourage others this week?

4. Do you see a need in your local church for more discussions on sexual sin and discipleship in this area? Consider sharing this resource with your pastors or other church members that would benefit from it.

KEY SCRIPTURES

- Matthew 5:8
- John 15:11
- John 16:22
- Ephesians 2:10
- Galatians 6:2
- 1 Corinthians 6
- Psalm 16:1-2

RECOMMENDED RESOURCES

- *Pure in Heart* by Garrett Kell
- *What is the Meaning of Sex* by Denny Burk
- *Making All Things New* by David Powlison
- Get a discount on Accountable2You using the link: a2u.app/IntoTheLight
- Get a discount on Covenant Eyes using the code: INTOTHELIGHT
- Other Into The Light Resources: intothelightministries.ca

Pornography And Missions

Bonus Chapter – David Platt

Group Study: Week 7

START HERE

In this bonus chapter, David Platt speaks on pornography's ramifications for missions and evangelism. He also speaks on how freedom from pornography is not intended to stop with you; it is meant to spread through you.

Before watching the episode, **take time to open in prayer and read the following passages**:

> Revelation 7:9–12
> "After this I looked, and behold, a great multitude that no one could number, from every nation, from all tribes and peoples and languages, standing before the throne and before the Lamb, clothed in white robes, with palm branches in their hands, and crying out with a loud voice, "Salvation belongs to our God who sits on the throne, and to the Lamb!" And all the angels were standing around the throne and around the elders and the four living creatures, and they fell on their faces before the throne and worshiped God, saying, "Amen! Blessing and glory and wisdom and thanksgiving and honor and power and might be to our God forever and ever! Amen.""

> Matthew 28:18–20
> "Jesus came and said to them, "All authority in heaven and on earth has been given to me. Go therefore and make disciples of all nations, baptizing them in the name of the Father and of the Son and of the Holy Spirit, teaching them to observe all that I have commanded you. And behold, I am with you always, to the end of the age.""

SCAN TO WATCH

intothelightministries.ca

KEY IDEAS

1. God made us to enjoy him and exalt his name among all nations.

2. God's global mission is not only for "special individuals" but for every Christian in Christ's church.

3. Porn is a weapon of Satan to keep the nations from hearing the good news.

4. The consequences of personal sin reach farther than the individual; it impacts God's kingdom.

5. Your freedom is not intended to stop with you; it is intended to spread through you.

NOTES

GROUP STUDY QUESTIONS

1. What is one thing that encouraged or challenged you from David's talk?

2. Re-read the Great Commission. How does your personal holiness affect Jesus's call for his people to make disciples, baptize them, and teach them his commandments?

> **Matthew 28:18–20**
> "Jesus came and said to them, "All authority in heaven and on earth has been given to me. Go therefore and make disciples of all nations, baptizing them in the name of the Father and of the Son and of the Holy Spirit, teaching them to observe all that I have commanded you. And behold, I am with you always, to the end of the age.""

3. David explained that billions of people have no access to beholding the glories of God and the gospel. How does this truth make you feel? How might this reality shape how you live your life?

4. Are you able to see how sin can blind you from the ways in which God wants to use you for the expansion of his kingdom? What are some of the profound kingdom impacts that could come from victory over this sin in your life?

5. How has this series/study impacted your fight against pornography? What was one of the biggest "aha" moments?

6. Who do you think would benefit from this series? Would you consider sharing it with them?

7. Think of all the missionaries who have been disqualified from being sent overseas due to pornography addiction. Consider praying as a group for the Lord to help break people from this bondage and that more men and women will be sent out to nations.

TAKE HOME QUESTIONS FOR FURTHER REFLECTION

1. How can you become an active agent in God's mission of evangelism and discipleship?

2. Are you part of a biblical church where you can care for the spiritual well-being of others? How can you start to love others in your church and help them fight sexual sin?

3. Does anyone in your extended family (sibling, spouse, children, grandparents) struggle with pornography? Consider watching our other series, *Parenting & Pornography*.

4. Part of Into The Light Ministries' mission is to make resources like this available all over the world. This includes continuing to build free resources as well as translating them into multiple languages. Would you prayerfully consider giving to the ministry as a way to help Christians all over the world find freedom from sexual sin?

5. Would you be willing to share your story with us? Consider writing down a few things that particularly helped you and then sharing them on Into The Light's website contact box.

KEY SCRIPTURES

- Matthew 28:18-20
- Revelation 7:9-12
- Psalm 27
- Joshua 7:10-26
- 1 John 3:9

RECOMMENDED RESOURCES

- *Don't Hold Back* by David Platt
- *Missions: How the Local Church Goes Global* by Andy Johnson
- *Cross Conference (Free Videos):* crosscon.com/past-conferences
- *Radical Website (Free Resources):* radical.net
- Get a discount on Accountable2You using the link: a2u.app/IntoTheLight
- Get a discount on Covenant Eyes using the code: INTOTHELIGHT
- Other Into The Light Resources: intothelightministries.ca

Into The Light
MINISTRIES

Bonus Chapter 99

Next Steps

Thank you for using this workbook to dive deeper into the *Into The Light* Documentary. Were you helped by this material? Please share your story with us on our website (intothelightministries.ca) and consider giving back to make more free resources on biblical sexuality available. We pray that these tools will equip you and your church to delight in God's good design and fight sexual sin.

1. Parenting & Pornography:
   Roadmaps to Raising Children of Integrity

2. TechSafe:
   Tutorials for Protecting Every Device in Your Home

3. Into The Light:
   A Teaching Documentary and Video Series on Freedom from Pornography

4. The Into The Light Podcast:
   Interviews on Biblical Sexuality and the Christian Life

Made in the USA
Columbia, SC
15 April 2025